SCIENTISTS
AT
WORK

Chemists at Work

SARA HOWELL

Britannica®
Educational Publishing

IN ASSOCIATION WITH

ROSEN
EDUCATIONAL SERVICES

Published in 2018 by Britannica Educational Publishing (a trademark of Encyclopædia Britannica, Inc.) in association with The Rosen Publishing Group, Inc.
29 East 21st Street, New York, NY 10010

Distributed exclusively by Rosen Publishing.
To see additional Britannica Educational Publishing titles, go to rosenpublishing.com.

First Edition

Britannica Educational Publishing
J.E. Luebering: Executive Director, Core Editorial
Mary Rose McCudden: Editor, Britannica Student Encyclopedia

Rosen Publishing
Amelie von Zumbusch: Editor
Nelson Sá: Art Director
Nicole Russo-Duca: Designer
Cindy Reiman: Photography Manager
Nicole DiMella: Photo Researcher

Library of Congress Cataloging-in-Publication Data

Names: Howell, Sara, author.
Title: Chemists at work / Sara Howell.
Description: First edition. | New York : Britannica Educational Publishing in Association with Rosen Educational Services, 2018. | Series: Scientists at work | Audience: Grades 1 to 4. | Includes bibliographical references and index.
Identifiers: LCCN 2016058556 | ISBN 9781680487558 (library bound : alk. paper) | ISBN 9781680487534 (pbk. : alk. paper) | ISBN 9781680487541 (6-pack : alk. paper)
Subjects: LCSH: Chemists—Juvenile literature. | Chemistry—Vocational guidance—Juvenile literature. | CYAC: Vocational guidance.
Classification: LCC QD39.5 .H69 2018 | DDC 540.23—dc23
LC record available at https://lccn.loc.gov/2016058556

Manufactured in the United States of America

Contents

What Is Chemistry?

C hemistry is one of the major branches of science. People who work in chemistry are called chemists. Chemists study the substances that make up matter. Matter is everything that takes up space in the universe. Matter includes living things, such as a dog or a person, and nonliving things, such as a book or a chair. Chemists also study the changes that take place when substances are combined. These changes are called chemical reactions.

In addition, chemists create new substances. They have made plastics, fibers,

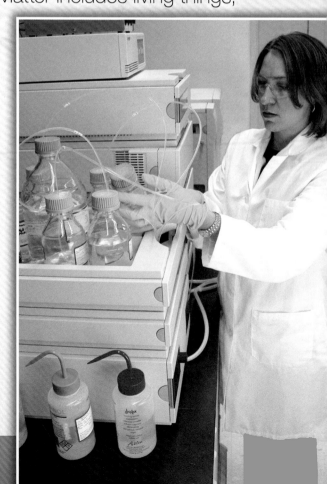

This chemist uses the tools in her laboratory to combine substances and observe when chemical reactions occur.

Plastic is a human-made material. There are many types of plastic. Most are made from chemicals that come from petroleum or coal.

building materials, medicines, and many other substances that are useful in everyday life. Like the substances chemists work with and study, a career in chemistry can take many different forms!

THINK ABOUT IT

Chemists have created many of the materials that we use in our lives every day. Look around you. What substances or materials do you see that were made possible by the work of chemists?

Elements and Compounds

Baking soda and vinegar are both compounds. When they are combined, a chemical reaction occurs.

The basic substances that chemists study are called chemical elements. Chemical elements are the building blocks for all matter. The smallest unit of an element is called an atom. Each element is made up of only one type of atom. Chemical reactions involve atoms or groups of atoms. When two or more atoms combine, they form a molecule.

Each element has certain properties. When elements are combined, they form a new substance with its own properties. A substance formed in this way is called a compound.

Table salt is a chemical compound. It is made up of equal parts of the elements sodium and chlorine.

There are a little more than 100 known elements. There are millions of compounds, though. A major part of a chemist's job is to study the way elements and compounds react and then develop new ways to use them.

THINK ABOUT IT

Water is a compound, made up of two elements called hydrogen and oxygen. How is water affected by high heat? How is it affected by extremely cold temperatures?

The Periodic Table

The periodic table is a system for arranging the chemical elements. Each chemical element has been assigned an atomic number. That number comes from the amount of tiny particles called **protons** in each atom of the element. For

The periodic table groups elements by their atomic numbers and their properties. There are ninety-two chemical elements found in nature. Scientists have created more than twenty additional elements.

Periodic Table of the Elements

H hydrogen
Fe iron
Ag silver
Au gold
C carbon **O** oxygen

Ia																	zero
1 H	IIa										IIIa	IVa	Va	VIa	VIIa		2 He
3 Li	4 Be	IIIb	IVb	Vb	VIb	VIIb		VIIIb		Ib	IIb	5 B	6 C	7 N	8 O	9 F	10 Ne
11 Na	12 Mg											13 Al	14 Si	15 P	16 S	17 Cl	18 Ar
19 K	20 Ca	21 Sc	22 Ti	23 V	24 Cr	25 Mn	26 Fe	27 Co	28 Ni	29 Cu	30 Zn	31 Ga	32 Ge	33 As	34 Se	35 Br	36 Kr
37 Rb	38 Sr	39 Y	40 Zr	41 Nb	42 Mo	43 Tc	44 Ru	45 Rh	46 Pd	47 Ag	48 Cd	49 In	50 Sn	51 Sb	52 Te	53 I	54 Xe
55 Cs	56 Ba	57 La	72 Hf	73 Ta	74 W	75 Re	76 Os	77 Ir	78 Pt	79 Au	80 Hg	81 Tl	82 Pb	83 Bi	84 Po	85 At	86 Rn
87 Fr	88 Ra	89 Ac	104 Rf	105 Db	106 Sg	107 Bh	108 Hs	109 Mt	110 Ds	111 Rg	112 Cn	113 Nh	114 Fl	115 Mc	116 Lv	117 Ts	118 Og

lanthanoid series	58 Ce	59 Pr	60 Nd	61 Pm	62 Sm	63 Eu	64 Gd	65 Tb	66 Dy	67 Ho	68 Er	69 Tm	70 Yb	71 Lu
actinoid series	90 Th	91 Pa	92 U	93 Np	94 Pu	95 Am	96 Cm	97 Bk	98 Cf	99 Es	100 Fm	101 Md	102 No	103 Lr

example, the element oxygen has an atomic number of 8 because each of its atoms has eight protons.

The periodic table arranges the elements in rows and columns. In the rows, the elements are placed in order of their atomic number. The columns form groups of elements that have similar chemical properties. For example, the group of gases known as the noble gases is in one column and metals called the alkali metals are in another. The periodic table helps chemists think about the elements and their properties.

A Russian chemist named Dmitry Mendeleyev developed the first periodic table in 1869.

Branches of Chemistry

Chemistry is a complex subject with many branches. For example, organic chemists deal only with compounds of the element carbon. Coal, plastic, rubber, and milk all contain carbon compounds.

Physical chemists measure the ways in which substances change during chemical reactions. Physical chemistry uses physics to study chemical problems and to provide a deeper understanding of chemistry.

Biochemists study chemical processes that happen in living things. The study of biochemistry has helped people in many

This bumblebee and honeysuckle plant both contain carbon compounds. Carbon compounds make up eighteen percent of all the matter in living things.

Special equipment allows biochemists to observe tiny particles such as atoms and molecules.

ways. Through the study of plants, biochemists have been able to increase the nutritional value of certain food crops. Scientists have been able to detect a wide variety of diseases by studying the chemical properties of blood. As they have learned how diseases work they have also been able to create new drugs to treat those diseases.

COMPARE AND CONTRAST

How are biochemists like other chemists? How are they different?

The Scientific Method

The process that chemists and other scientists use to solve problems is called the scientific method. Scientists start by finding out as much as possible about a problem. Then they make a hypothesis. A hypothesis is an attempt to explain the particular problem. Scientists then test the hypothesis with an experiment. If the experiment does not support the hypothesis, the scientists think about the problem again and develop a new hypothesis. They then test that hypothesis with a new experiment.

Chemists use the scientific method to test many hypotheses before they develop a scientific theory.

If the experiment supports the hypothesis, other scientists repeat the experiment to make sure that they get the same results. If they do get the same results, the hypothesis will be accepted as true until it can be proven false.

Scientists believe there is a natural explanation for most things. For any problem they see, they try to understand the cause so they can come up with a solution.

Scientists use the information they learn from testing many hypotheses to develop scientific theories. A scientific theory is a broad explanation for why things work or how things happen in the natural world.

COMPARE AND CONTRAST

How are a hypothesis and a theory different? How are they alike?

Chemists in Action

Chemistry involves many different areas of study. Even within the same field, though, the job of one chemist can be very different than the job of another. Chemists can work in many different fields, from law enforcement to the development of life-saving medicines and **vaccines**.

Forensic chemists work with law enforcement officers to analyze

VOCABULARY

Vaccines are substances that prevent the spread of disease. They are made from the same microbes that cause the diseases they are used to prevent.

This forensic chemist is analyzing a drug. Forensic chemists can help identify substances that are found at crime scenes.

evidence, such as blood traces, collected at crime scenes. They might also be called into court to testify about their findings. Environmental chemists study the effect of chemicals on the air, soil, and water. They monitor how pollution and waste from human activities affect the environment. Industrial chemists use chemical processes to develop new products such as cosmetics and plastics.

Industrial chemists often test products, such as the chlorine seen here, as they are being produced to make sure the chemical compounds are correct.

Education Needed

To pursue a career in chemistry, a person should earn a bachelor's degree from a college or university, which generally takes four years. With a bachelor's degree in chemistry, biochemistry, or another related field, a chemist can begin his or her career with an entry-level position such as laboratory technician.

For more advanced positions in chemistry, students can pursue advanced degrees. A master's degree can take

These students are learning to conduct experiments and record their findings in a college chemistry class.

an additional one or two years to earn. A PhD can then take anywhere from an additional four to seven years to complete.

Many chemists also join professional organizations such as the American Chemical Society. The organizations help them connect with other chemists, develop their skills, and find jobs.

THINK ABOUT IT

Students studying chemistry take classes in organic and inorganic chemistry, physics, and advanced mathematics, such as calculus. Why do you think it is important for chemists to understand advanced mathematical concepts?

Life in the Lab

Most chemists, regardless of their field, begin their careers working in research laboratories. A laboratory is a place equipped for making scientific experiments and tests. Many chemists continue to work and conduct their research at universities. Others, such as forensic chemists, work in laboratories operated by federal or local police departments or medical examiners offices.

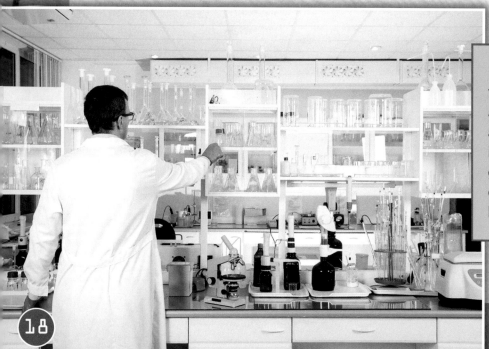

Laboratories that are well stocked will have all of the equipment a chemist needs, including beakers, graduated cylinders, droppers, and Bunsen burners.

Chemists study underground gases in an area of the Czech Republic that has experienced numerous earthquakes.

Not all chemists spend every day in a laboratory, though. Environmental chemists may spend some of their time outside taking water or soil samples. Chemists can also use their skills to run companies or to teach at high schools and colleges.

THINK ABOUT IT

Chemists often work as part of a team while conducting research and experiments. Can you think of any ways working as a group might be helpful or more difficult than working individually?

Chemistry Toolkit

Laboratories are filled with the tools chemists need to perform experiments, from test tubes and thermometers to safety equipment such as goggles. One key tool is a microscope.

Scientists use microscopes to see objects that are too small to be seen with the eye alone. Such objects include cells, tiny living things, and grains of sand.

There are several types of microscopes. **Optical** microscopes, also called light microscopes, use lenses, which are

Safety equipment is very important in a lab. Chemists often work with substances that can be dangerous if they get in the eyes or on the skin.

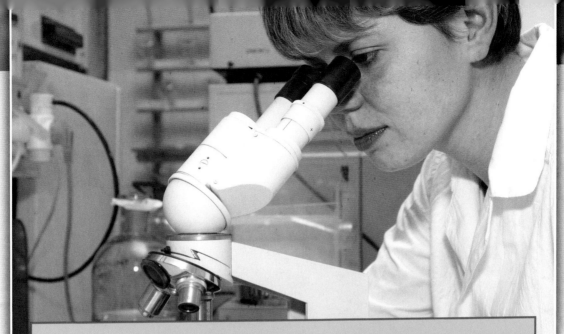

Optical microscopes often come with multiple objective lenses with different magnifications. An objective lens is a lens near the object being viewed. This microscope has three objective lenses that can be rotated.

curved pieces of glass or plastic that bend light. The object to be studied sits under a lens. As light passes from the object through the lens, the lens makes the object look bigger.

To view small objects even more closely, scientists use electron microscopes. These microscopes use beams of electrons instead of light to magnify objects. Electrons are some of the particles that make up atoms.

History of Chemistry

Chemistry has many modern applications and uses. As a field of study, though, chemistry is hundreds of years old. People first studied chemistry as a science in the seventeenth century. In 1661 a British scientist named Robert Boyle published a book describing chemical elements as simple, basic substances. In the 1770s a French chemist named Antoine Lavoisier helped to explain chemical reactions.

Antoine Lavoisier showed that the process of breathing is similar to the chemical reaction that takes place when something is burned. In both cases there is a reaction involving the chemical element oxygen.

In the early 1800s a British chemist named John Dalton found that each element has its own kind of atom. Other chemists discovered many new elements during the 1800s. Later chemists continued to make discoveries about atoms. For example, they learned that atoms are made up of even simpler particles. Each new discovery made by chemists has built upon the ones before it.

John Dalton also made important discoveries in the field of meteorology (or the study of weather) and the study of color blindness.

Famous Chemists

One of the most famous chemists in history was Louis Pasteur. He lived in the 1800s in France. Pasteur discovered that fermentation involved tiny germs called microbes.

Fermentation is a chemical change used to make bread, wine, cheese, and other foods. Pasteur showed that heat kills the microbes that cause fermentation. This discovery led him to invent a process for destroying harmful microbes in food. This process became known as pasteurization. It slows down the spoiling of food. Pasteurization is still used today. Pasteur also discovered

The process that Pasteur developed for destroying harmful microbes in food is still used today.

Marie Curie won the Nobel Prize for Physics in 1903 and the Nobel Prize for Chemistry in 1911. She is the only woman in history to have won the prize in two different fields.

VOCABULARY

Radioactivity is a feature of certain elements. Atoms of those elements change over time and release energy and small particles.

that many diseases are caused by microbes. He developed vaccines as a method of preventing disease.

The work of the Polish-French scientist Marie Curie focused on **radioactivity**. Curie helped to discover two radioactive elements, polonium and radium. Radium was used for many years to treat cancer. In 1911 Curie won the Nobel Prize for Chemistry for isolating pure radium.

25

Future Challenges

Many advances have been made in the field of chemistry over the last century, but there are still many questions left to answer about how elements and chemicals work. Today's chemists are working to find cures for diseases, such as cancer, as well as to develop new vaccines. Chemists are developing plant-based fuels and plastics to move away from a dependence on fossil fuels, such as oil. Fossil fuels are the remains of things that lived long ago. Earth has a limited supply

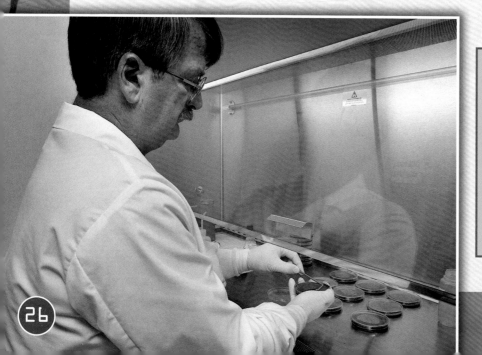

Chemists working at the Centers for Disease Control research different strains of bacteria that can be dangerous to the public health.

Chemists are developing new ways to create fuels from plant material. This biofuel was produced using Napier grass. The grass is also known as elephant grass or Uganda grass.

of them. They cannot be replaced once they are used up.

As technology evolves, chemists will have better tools to investigate problems and perform experiments. For example, as computers get more powerful, chemists can use them to collect and analyze huge amounts of data in a much shorter amount of time.

COMPARE AND CONTRAST

Biofuels are made from plant or animal materials. For example, ethanol is made from corn. How is ethanol like fossil fuels? How is it different?

A Dynamic Career

Have you ever considered working in the field of chemistry? Chemistry deals with the **composition**, structure, and properties of substances and with the changes that they go through. This may seem very broad. What it means, though, is that chemistry can offer an exciting career, no matter what your other interests are. Maybe you would like to save lives or save the environment. Maybe you would like to

A simple home chemistry set may help you get interested in learning more about chemistry.